How To Successfully Use Lean
Sigma In Your Business to
Give You The
Competitive Edge

by Robert Potter

How to Successfully Use Lean Sigma in Your Business to Give You the Competitive Edge

ISBN-13: 978-1484904671

ISBN-10: 1484904672

Contents

Introduction

Why is Lean Sigma (or Lean Thinking) so prevalent in the current economy? For a company to remain a competitive, agile, cost-efficient and streamlined business, getting rid of waste, along with consistency and sustainability are key for survival and growth in this new economy.

Lean Sigma is exactly as the name implies – it is about 'cut to the bone', fat-trimmed, streamlining of operations and organisations.

Authors Womack and Jones define Lean Sigma as "A set or collection of 'efficiency tools' that you can unleash in your business to save money, reduce cost and waste to deliver consistent, effective service that is affordable and pleasing to your customers".

It is about vision and tools for reducing inconsistency and cutting down on waste, being efficient and running a smooth, competitive, profitable operation.

The Japanese motor giant Toyota is often thought to be the originator of Lean Sigma. Whilst it is true that Lean Sigma was eventually adopted by the Japanese automakers as the principle upon which they wanted to build, run and grow their businesses, the actual origin of the modern Lean Sigma principles can be traced back to the work of W. Edwards Deming and Walter A. Shewhart and their work in the area of total quality management.

It is worth noting that total quality management principles began their development in May 1924 with Shewhart and have been evolving ever since. The American Deming has been honored in Japan for being the inspirational driving force that rebuilt Toyota into the high quality Lean Sigma company it is today. When the Lean Sigma concept was re-introduced to the West, it made its reappearance as a Japanese idea, complete with Japanese terms for its different parts. The Western world has been quick to embrace the value and potential of this approach to organisations and operations.

What is Lean Sigma?

Some have referred to Lean Sigma as the Toyota Production System, or JIT (just-in-time). However, looking more closely, we see that it originated in the Bell Corporation in the US before Deming brought it to Japan. Lean Sigma is all about paying close attention to flow productions, line operations and value streams of all kinds, so it is very suitable for financial services in pretty much any organisation . This is known as Kaizen.

In any lean approach, there are certain key things to pay attention to. There are discipline, planning, scientific approach and statistically based tools required and applied to make this business paradigm fit, work and last.

How Lean Sigma helps business processes, results and success

Lean Sigma will help you to take a serious look at visible causes and their effects on your business. Aspects to focus on include:

Inventory
Movement/motion
Waiting or queues
Broken machines or tools (missing)
Dirt and clutter
Noise
Untapped resources

… and many others.

Different types of waste (MUDA)

Obvious observable waste or inefficiencies attract attention and demand action. This is where Lean Sigma can make the difference between being efficient or not. It deals with the problems that we can actually see and do something about.

True to its newfound Japanese "origin", there is lots of "legacy" terminology here; one of those terms is MOST appropriate as we start discussing lean tools and their implications for your business:

It is referred to as MUDA, essentially meaning WASTE. In any process and business, there are nine forms of MUDA/WASTE:

Making products, delivering service that no one wants OR NOT MEETING USER NEEDS (useless) DEFECTIVE products or flawed services (mistakes)

Making too much of something (overproduction)
Inventory
Unnecessary processing (non-value added steps)
Unnecessary movement of people
Unnecessary movement of things
Waiting or queuing
Not paying attention to front line staff

What does Lean Sigma bring to business?

There are many reasons people would want to use Lean Sigma principles in their organisation or business including:

Breakthrough performance
Increased quality
Shorter cycle times
Creating shareholder value
Applying the principles throughout every level of the organisation

When you focus on any improvements for efficiency and profit, you will have to pay attention to the sayings "time is money" and "quality matters". These two principles and fundamental pillars for Lean Sigma will reward you greatly if considered in all aspects and areas of your business.

Achieve cost reductions on your terms
Cut lead/wait times within a short period of time, in a planned fashion using lean tools to get you there. Cut down on processing time from start to finish, from the moment the order is placed to when it is shipped and delivered. (Also referred to as cycle time).

What are the value propositions of Lean Sigma?

Value: When a product or service has been perceived or appraised to fulfil a need or desire ... as defined by the Customer - the product or service may be said to have value or worth.

Value Adding: The creation of value through waste-free operations and processes. Any operation or activity that changes, converts or transforms materials or information into a product or service the customer is willing to pay for.

Non-Value Adding: Any operation or activity that takes time and resources, but does not add value to the product or service for the Customer (Waste)

Through using Lean Sigma, you can combine business improvement with business strategy. You will need both to be successful and get results that last.

There are ways that you can decide which specific approach or major projects can have the MOST impact on your bottom line, strategy and overall financial priorities.

Eliminate delays, waiting times, obstacles, bottlenecks and unnecessary waste hindering expedient, reliable, efficient and affordable products and services.

> Removing non-value add is at the very heart of Lean Sigma thinking, directly leading to significant cost savings. It is a philosophy and a practical business strategy that will greatly reward businesses and increase shareholder value significantly.

These tools complement and reinforce efficiency and streamlined lean sigma operations, with measurable returns to your pocket and bottom line – the main reason for being in business in the first place.

In a time when businesses have to keep up with all the constant change around them, agility and adaptability are key. Everyone is talking about the "organic", collaborative workplace where we all work well together towards mutual goals. This may sound uncomfortable, however a work force that feels a sense of belonging is far more efficient than an insecure one. You also need to know your staff. If you have an office of engineers and you tell them you want an organic, collaborative workplace, you may just scare them all into leaving.

When introducing change you have to sell it to your staff, and that involves getting to know their needs and pitching it to them, as you would sell product to your customers.

Business, transactional and production efficiencies are essential parts of success, processes and outcomes that will serve and enable all of the above.

- There is the definite potential to significantly cut costs and waste, be more efficient and increase shareholder value and profits.
- Tools, utilities and processes are needed to affect these outcomes.

- These approaches and tools can help you leverage and position your business to stand out from the crowd when it comes to quality.

Lean Sigma has helped an increasing list of big companies like GE and Toyota to lower costs, cut waste and improve how they utilise their resources, quality and time. The question you need to ask in your own business is "what are you leveraging to keep your company competitive?'

If you are paying close attention to time and quality in your business, then Lean Sigma is the tool for you. Those businesses that don't pay attention to the crucial elements of time and quality may continue to struggle, and are unlikely to survive in the long term.

Reducing waiting times, bottlenecks, cycles and lead times all matter to both the business and the customer. Variation in the time it takes to complete any given process (or steps within a process) causes an inconsistent customer experience. This has to be dealt with to ensure customer satisfaction.

A typical example would be delivery 'windows' and managing expectations around them. Lean Sigma is about more than identifying and dealing with defects. It goes beyond cause and effect and aims to identify and eliminate the gremlins in the system that have the potential to cause damage.

The reliability of your operations and business to your customers should be a top priority. Lean Sigma thinking, approaches and tools can help you achieve this.

In this new economy, both speed and reliability makes the difference. What was the gold standard yesterday quickly becomes the entry-level requirement and pre-requisite in a highly competitive market. To stay on top, you need to be able to adjust and deliver consistently. This means you and your business have to continually change and improve. Lean Sigma (a combination of Lean and Six Sigma tools) is not a one-time fix - it's a set of tools, that when used correctly, will help you to change quickly and effectively; so that your business is the one others try to emulate.

> Reducing overhead NVA cost and inventory is at the heart of Lean Sigma.

Two business metrics that are oftentimes used to measure a business' performance are:

1. On-time delivery of service or product
2. Reduction in lead-time for the service or product.

Time and quality often suffer in a fast-paced business, yet today's consumers are increasingly demanding and insisting on both as a basic service. This expectation will only increase into the future.

Typically, companies embrace change at a slow pace. Change takes time. Lean Sigma turbo-charges these improvement efforts and underpins the processes and outcomes undertaken.

Simply put, high quality, high speed and low cost are the outcomes you are after with lean tools, thinking and processes.

If you are after sustained value creation in your business, then Lean Sigma can provide the answer and solution for you. This is often found in combination with process and business improvement tools like Six Sigma.

Lean Sigma processes can sometimes appear to be quite counter-intuitive, but it would be a mistake to think that applying simplistic methods and wisdom to process and outcome would fail. There are countless examples of companies, both large and small, that have used these tried and tested methodologies with great success.

> Lean Sigma requires a strong sense of leadership, and leading by example will be required.
> "Toyota managers should be sufficiently engaged on the factory floor that they have to wash their hands at least **three times a day**."
> -Taiichi Ohno

Optimising opportunity is the name of the game with Lean. Moving faster and with quality in mind, lowering cost and any wastage in the process will have you reaping rewards in no time. This can give you a real competitive edge.

Many have defined Lean Sigma as "the streamlining of business processes to get the most out of equipment, inventory, and people".

To keep things really simple, Lean Sigma has a base premise and overall goal 'to get more done with less'

This is achieved by

   i.   Minimising inventory
   ii.   At and through all stages of the service or production
   iii.   Eliminating waste
   iv.   Reducing wait times, queues
   v.   Shortening cycle times from raw materials to finished goods
   vi.   Improving and streamlining business processes

Benefits of Lean Sigma

Lean Sigma processes involve tangible, positive, productive changes in businesses that will have a measurable impact on your bottom line.

Benefits of Lean Sigma include:

- o Reduced lead time, wait time and cycle time
- o Liberated capital
- o Increased profit margins
- o Increased productivity
- o Improved product quality
- o Just-in-time, affordable, streamlined, cost-efficient processes, products and services
- o Improved on-time shipments
- o Customer satisfaction and loyalty
- o Employee retention (the right ones)

Lean Sigma affords you the opportunity to ensure your business grows stronger, quicker and consistently, while getting higher value and improving competitiveness. The difference this makes can effectively position your business way out in front of your competition.

Lean Sigma is an on-going process. This approach and paradigm focusing on time and quality, while reducing cost and waste and streamlining operations can assist you in reducing inventories, work-in-process (often referred to as WIP), required floor space, cycle times and lead times.

Lean Sigma (especially when combined with business improvement efforts such as Six Sigma methods and disciplines) can lead to tangible, measurable improvements. Most of the tools focus on really simple concepts and are easy to use and implement. Lean Sigma focuses on the visible; what you can see, change and control. It connects steps, processes and people. It spots waste and problems and allows us all to identify, spot and deal with errors quicker and more effectively, saving more money in the process.

There is nothing really complex or mysterious about it. Anyone can apply it to their business, no matter what industry they are in. It does not have to be complicated or only accessible by the chosen few. It can be a great tool to mobilise your organisation.

A simple business strategy

Product Leadership
Offering the best Products/Services by focusing on Innovation and Value

Customer Intimacy
Cultivating lasting relationships and striving to satisfy their unique needs.

Operational Excellence
Providing products and services at the lowest cost, highest quality/compliance and with the greatest efficiency.

Lean Tools to use in your business

The basic toolkit of Lean Sigma has tools that will consistently and constantly enable you to change ineffective processes to smoothly operating and flowing production lines. It provides everyone the opportunity to 'take control' and have pride in the work that they do. It is a hands-on enabler. When people understand how and what affects process and outcome and take a cause/effect, analytical approach to things around them, such as work processes for example, a whole new world of understanding, accountability and change comes into being. It re-energises your business, and when the rewards start trickling in, everyone can share in the success and results.

One myth that needs dispelling right off the bat is that Lean Sigma is only for high-volume or standardised processes. This is far from the truth. Lean Sigma is versatile and robust enough to be applied in any context on any system or process in numerous forms. If we consider Lean Sigma qualifies in manufacturing, batch operations, mixed model production systems, shift-by-shift changes, switching of dyes, etc. Whether you are making appliances, light bulbs, providing a service or niche product, Lean Sigma can be applied to help you in all aspects of your business, including financial, transactional, ordering, inventory and HR processes (payroll, hiring etc.)

You pick your priority: Streamlining operations, improving productivity, eliminating waste; whichever it is, Lean Sigma has a tool for that.

Here are some steps in the Lean Sigma process to consider for your business if you are contemplating taking a real hard look at how you operate, function and plan to get better using Lean tools:

Steps in the Lean Sigma process

Step 1: Leadership and Commitment

Buying in, championing and supporting the effort from the top is essential. Decision-makers have to back up what is being planned and visibly support the improvement efforts and projects. Without this support, companies will often quickly revert back to old habits and sustained change will not be possible nor feasible.

Vision and direction has to come from senior management as well. In addition to buying in, you need to plan its introduction, so the staff doesn't see it as the latest hobby-horse of the owner that they fully expect to fall out of favour eventually.

Step 2: Educate and Empower: Gather knowledge and know-how and practice Lean Sigma

Training, fundamentals and even books, consulting and advice from other businesses that are implementing and experimenting with Lean can all help you get on your way.

It is a priority to educate and empower, giving people the tools they need, raising awareness of Lean, introducing and using a couple of the tools at a time over a period of a couple of weeks or months with a whole coordinated deployment or roll-out effort with resources and project plans. These are all feasible, depending on the needs of your organisation and the depth you want to or feel like you have to go into.

Step 3: Making Things Visible To All and Accountability

It's important to note that if your staff is not performing as desired; there are issues with the process, not the staff.

Understanding processes such as cause and effect, root-cause analysis and even being aware of waste goes a long way to get to the low-hanging fruit, the win and the reward right away. Any improvement for your business - saving money and lower costs - has to be a good result. This is the best reason to use Lean to help you and your employees see and do something about it.

Try to see if you can trace the source of waste. Just walk around your operation and see if you can spot where 'waste' is occurring. Are there any discarded, defective products, things on the floor or cluttered areas? This exercise can be a great first step. Try tracing and mapping out how it got there, and deducing how severe the problem is (pages per day, waste removed or scrapped, defective unit number versus yield). Any metrics and active tracking heightens awareness of potential problems and sources. All wonderful, without necessarily even having implemented any formal Lean Tools as yet. See the promise and potential here?

This can very easily become the base or platform for identifying bottlenecks, excess inventory and even discontinuous flow. Getting all the staff involved in these processes will give you a great opportunity to motivate and mobilise your entire workforce.

Step 4: Focused Improvement Activities and Advanced Lean Tools

Map out the major processes in your business. Identify all the sources of waste and prioritise the areas you want to focus on first, where the maximum gain is with minimum effort. Take the area, process or problem apart, analyse it and see how you can make it better. Put the improvements in place and ensure that it does not happen again.

It's important to ensure that the progress you make in this area is not temporary. Plan for its sustainability by having a project or process champion and getting employees to take the lead and responsibility as well.

Some of the most wonderful stories, opportunities and promise lie in the fact that Lean Sigma effectively brings together a motivated group of individuals involved in work and/or a typical process including people from other areas of an operation to combine their talents and focus on a particular issue, topic, area or problem.

Next, define and map the current situation's cost and waste, (baseline and diagnose), then set some clear objectives to change and make things better. These can be metrics or stated smart goals measured in terms of wait or lead-time, process steps, cycle time, floor-space, inventory and other metrics.

A time frame for improvements is set, and the group celebrates the successes, outcomes and results together.

Step 5: Looking Further Ahead and Beyond

Lean Sigma enables you to get renewed momentum, continued effort and ongoing improvement individually, collectively and as an organisation (what Lean often refers to as Kaizen – the pursuit of continual improvement and perfection ... a standard of sorts).

Lean Sigma tools

Some of the Lean Sigma tools that might be able to help you in your processes are:

5S
Cellular Processing
Mistake Proofing
Set-Up Reduction
Failure Mode and Effect Analysis

A basic, fundamental tool in Lean Sigma that can help any business, the '5S' approach is an organising, and structuring technique to get rid of clutter and waste. Cleanliness and having a set place for everything are key to achieving this.

5S
The name stems from the Japanese meanings and equivalent words for:

Sorting things (Seiri)
Setting things in a particular order (Seiton)
Shining, daily maintenance (Seiso)
Standardisation (Seiketsu)
Sustainability (Shitsuke)

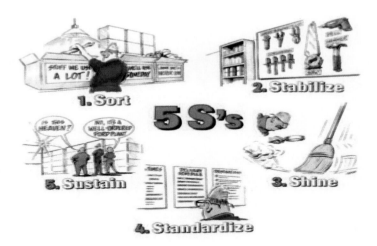

You can increase your efficiency and reduce waste by applying these tools to your business.

Cellular Processing
Cellular processing has to do with organising not only the workplace, but also the work. Workcells and designated work areas, along with certain spaces for certain activities, minimise movement of people and things and therefore cost less. In an operational sense, this means no batching, no waiting, no delays, no queuing, just smooth operation and easy flow.

Mistake-proofing (Poka-Yoke)
Built-in safeguards and reducing defects to zero are at the centre of this approach. Highlighting problems as they occur, not permitting mistakes, oversights and errors to slip through are key. Processes are designed around this principle to be more efficient

and will help your business cut down on cost, scrap and waste.

Error Proofing - Others

Seat belt warning light/buzzer

Petrol/gas pumps size & color

Automatic Washroom

Egg Carton

Lawn mower two hand start

Drop Down Menus

Set-up Reduction

SMED (Single-Minute Exchange of Die): Quick and speedy change over in business processes and operations are essential. Remember time and quality matter and mean money. Process thinking is the key here. Getting rid of unnecessary steps, actions or movement are also key. Reducing time on any line makes you more efficient and saves money.

There is more to Lean Sigma than these tools. They just serve as an indicator to some of the major business enablers that Lean Sigma can bring to your business and organisation.

TWO KEY REWARDS FOR YOUR BUSINESS TO
CAPITALISE ON: Breakthrough profit and
competitive advantage

Improving quality and speedy delivery rates are any
company's priorities. Making and keeping customers
happy is what it is all about. Lean Sigma offers you
the tools to do that practically, quickly, easily and
consistently.

You cannot change what you do not acknowledge or
know about. Lean Sigma comes with the appeal and
awareness to 'take note' and notice things around
you (cost, waste, movement, clutter, scrap, etc.) and
then DO something real, meaningful and constructive
about them.

Questions, diagnostics and assessments

What improvements should and could be made are
both important questions to ask, prioritise and act
upon. Customer priorities, things that affect your
incoming revenue should get attention quickly and as
a priority. Things like quality, lead and waiting times,
cycle time, cost, inventory and other internal
processes that affect the customer and are 'internal'
and controllable should be identified and dealt with
expediently.

Customer Needs - Kano Model

Here are some ideas to get you started asking the right type of questions to provide you with hints as to a strategy and starting point/priority:

- Which process or step should get the bulk of our immediate attention – where is the biggest WIN-WIN for both the customer and the company?

- What are all the priorities that we need to pay attention to in this organisation? Map the processes and make the list. Then ask, in what order should you tackle the priorities?

- How do we get the BEST improvements quickly? How do/can we tap into the benefits of Lean Sigma right away?

If reducing overhead, quality costs and inventory to save money, reducing waste and being a smooth-operating, streamlined and cost-efficient provider are keys to your business success, Lean Sigma can help you in all aspects and areas.

Taking the theory of Lean Sigma to practical implementation will take planning, patience and persistence as well as determination, detail orientation and discipline.

These are often referred to as the three P's and the three D's to make them easy to remember. Gradual, planned, focused effort is what it is all about. Step-by-step instructions and actions to get to improvements over time that can be sustained, stable and predictable are essential.

Operational and economic benefits

If any of the following scenarios are important to your business, Lean Sigma can help you reach targets and goals that you set for yourself, your team and your business:

- Increasing operating margin and revenue
- Reduce process lead, wait and cycle times
- Lessen WIP (work-in-progress) inventory (i.e. half-completed product), time and space costs money. Reduce costs
- Reducing overhead and quality costs
- Increase gross profit margin

- Get customers what they want, when they want it, anytime, every time and all the time, quickly and correctly, affordably and on demand.
- Achieve consistent quality and a low defect rate (scrap/waste)

Make the most of your shareholder value and you cannot go wrong. Achieve high levels of improvement rates and customer satisfaction, quality products, low costs and do so quickly so you can remain competitive and profitable.

Get and keep your processes under control and make sure you are getting better all the time, setting and positioning yourself head-and-shoulders above your competition. Help define and execute your competitive edge with a well thought out, supported, gradual deployment, throughout of Lean Sigma in your business and you are set for desired outcomes, success and results.

Having a very real, measurable impact and resulting dramatic improvements in your business and listening to your customer complaints can give you great hints as to where some of the problems might lie. DO NOT hesitate to ASK your customers, they will tell you. It is a wonderful opportunity and channel to let your customers know that what they want, say and need, really matters. If you provide this level of responsive personalised business, you will have success, not only now, but also in the future.

Slow and inefficient processes, finished goods just sitting around or waiting for things to happen all cost money.

Finding ways to cut down on these is the challenge and opportunity that Lean Sigma brings to your business. This is often referred to as the 'hidden factory' or 'unseen cost of doing business'. Once you put a number on it and are aware of it, you will benefit from ways to reduce or eliminate it, adding to your bottom line and cutting down on cost and waste. That is the heart and purpose of Lean Sigma.

Getting rid of things (even internal process steps, time and inventory) that add no value to your customers is a top priority, too. The cost of poor quality products, services and waste add up over time and could cause you your competitive edge and the loss of the loyalty and potential repeat/new business of your customers. Really taking issues with these aspects can save you time and money, and ensure quality and customer retention, satisfaction and more business.

Customers want to do more business with a provider that is reliable, quick, affordable, stable and predictable.
If you set certain targets in certain areas of your business and work diligently towards them, the results will be evident quickly and these changes will 'stick' and be sustainable over time. This is the real result you are aiming for.

Ask yourself how long it takes you to get your product or service to your customer. Seconds, minutes, hours, days, weeks? Asking the question is important as it raises your awareness. Putting a number to it makes it visible and measurable and enables you to do something about it. For example, a target would be to cut this time down by a quantifiable amount.

Any and all processes within your business need to come under this level of scrutiny. No exceptions. Other examples could easily include: Product development, order entries, design, customer service, HR and financial processes as well.

By taking this 'overall' holistic approach to improving your business in all areas and aspects means you are in effect adding value to your business, growing your profits and bottom line, while streamlining and becoming a smooth, low-cost, predictable partner and provider of choice.

Taking an analytical approach to business in this fashion opens your eyes to new channels and ways to grow and expand, strengthen and position your business for success and results.

Ask the following questions to ascertain if Lean Sigma is right and holds potential for you and your business:

- Where is the real 'time' in our business spent? How much of this adds value to our customers? Is it worth it? Where can we make some changes?

- Is there any benefit in our business trying to establish a competitive edge getting goods and services to customers quicker?

- What kind of payback can we expect from these Lean Sigma efforts? What are the financial gains and potential here?

- If we cut operating expenses, costs, overhead, inventory, lead, wait and cycle times, how would it affect the bottom line? What would the €€ impact be weekly, monthly, quarterly, annually? Again, these metrics will help you gauge your progress, raise awareness and give you a whole new outlook on what your business is doing well and what the areas for improvement are.

- If we reduce our goods in waiting and finished goods inventories, what will that mean in quantifiable monetary terms to our business? What would we be able to do with the cash at hand (investment, debt reduction, new machinery, marketing, etc.)? How can these changes, and Euros saved BEST benefit and grow your business?

In any Lean Sigma deployment and change management or improvement initiative in your business, there are enabling aspects to pay attention to:

Some of the operational and economic benefits or metrics to look out for to help you answer some/any of the above are:

- Operating margin
- ROIC (Return On Investment Capital)
- EBITDA (Earnings Before Interest, Taxes, Depreciation and Amorisation)
- Capital turnover
- WIP
- On-time delivery rates and ratios
- Cost of poor quality
- Quality performance, customer satisfaction data

If you have your focus set on the top spot in your industry, expanding your markets and horizons and increasing your market share, this is the way to go about it quickly, reliably and with sustainable gains.

There is a simple rule of thumb here, central to all of Lean Sigma as well, any improvements made within your business should benefit your customers and add value.

Lean Sigma succeeds in making the time, quality and cost issues within and between processes visible and tangible. It gives eyes and ears to these processes, outcomes and allows you to do something meaningful and intervene to make things better, to the benefit of your company and customers. It provides purpose, direction, baseline and practical means to get your results - and effect changes for good.

Lean is a seamless operation and less bureaucratic. It streamlines effective processes that make business successful. This overall business methodology and thinking will help you re-make, energise and shape your business better. You are now pro-active and hands-on in your operation, not leaving success up to random chance, but rather planning and executing for it.

> A GOLDEN RULE OF LEAN:
> Slow processes are expensive. Lean Sigma helps you to speed things up without sacrificing quality.

Agility, adaptability, low cost and responsiveness are all qualities that business should have and desperately need as prerequisites and entry requirements for doing business in the new economy.

One of the great contributions that Lean Sigma can/does make to your business is what we will refer to as 'shared purpose, direction and goals'. This individual and mutual 'orientation' and 'coordinated effort gives common direction to all, fosters commitment and camaraderie. It strengthens and builds the organisation, links the leaders to the shop floor employees and engages everyone at all levels to achieve better consistently.

It is a unifying and motivational principle that will underpin and build your efforts, getting you results quicker and maintaining it over time. Making success stick, so to speak.

So, ask yourself first and foremost how you think Lean Sigma can help you in your business, consider your options, pros and cons of doing/not doing it and then make your decision.

Enable and strengthen your business by using Lean Sigma tools to drive improvements, cost reduction and implement it across the levels and aspects of your business that matters most and reaps the highest rewards quickly.

Other aspects of lean to consider for Lean Sigma deployment in your business are as follows:

Leadership

Initiative and leading by example from the top is key. The main flag-bearer and champion of this Lean Sigma process and initiative starts with the business leader (CEO/President) and the senior management team. This is crucial as buy-in and support can make or break the efforts of Lean Sigma.

Personal, hands-on, practical engagement, commitment, practice and even rewards for full participation in these initiatives, being the drivers of performance per se are critical to and for Lean Sigma success. Inspire and mobilise others.

Corporate, business culture and infrastructure, support and championing of the Lean Sigma efforts contribute to the momentum and success of it throughout the organisation.

Include and engage everyone. Lean Sigma provides you the opportunity to harness and leverage the talents of the entire workforce and collective, not merely a handful of individuals or employees. Make everyone count and contribute.

If lasting results and sustained top performance matter to you and your business, here are the means to that end in the Lean Sigma toolkit.

Metrics and goals make things easier to achieve and practically act upon, effect, change, impact, reshape, etc. Every aspect of your business needs to come under the spotlight.

Infrastructure, support and deployment

Share the commitment, discipline and persistent toil to get to where you need to be. It starts with everyone, not just some, and this is important to get across. Have your customer's frame-of-mind at every step, process and corner of what you are doing, planning and improving. Know what they value, why and how to get it to them quickly, effectively, consistently and affordably, anytime, every time. This is where your focus and the focus of everyone within your organisation needs to be.

Shareholder value and financial impact are good guidelines for priorities and activity within Lean Sigma. Improvements need to be measured and tracked.

Engage everyone in the process, assign roles and responsibilities and tap into the full potential everyone has to bring to the table. Committed resources, time and training (initial investment) will pay off quickly. Mobilise your workforce and enable, empower and energise them.

Vision

Making it all about our customers is key. They are responsible for your incoming revenue streams, they keep the wheels of your business turning. Quality, time, what they want and when they want it can make the difference between success and failure for your business. Reducing variability is essential. Be consistent, predictable and reliable as a provider and/or supplier or business partner and make what they want your priority. Never merely focus on reducing defects, also know why you are doing it and how it adds value to your customers.

Everyone in your business has to understand this undertaking, its value and potential and the role, contribution and recognition of their efforts and input.

Right resources and projects

Having dedicated resources working tirelessly and exclusively on Lean Sigma-type processes and work, improvements and projects will give you your desired outcomes. For meaningful performance improvement, you need the right people and the right projects, working on the right value-added things within your business. Focused, deliberately targeted WORK is essential for results and success.

Teamwork

It is about everyone's roles and responsibilities. All matter. Leaders, shop, floor, administrative, all staff can contribute and make a difference. Leaders often mount the charge and get the ball rolling, providing support and encouragement along the way. Direction and results matter here.

Company	Ideas per employee per year
Toyota	33
Lexus	100
Milliken	110
Aisen Seiki	225 (in year 1983)
Boardroom Inc. USA	104 (in year 2002)
Richter Sounds	20
Dana Corp. USA	20-25
C2 Management, Sweden	60
Coca Cola Sweden, Production department	15
Porsche, Germany	12 (1996)

Full-time sponsors, champions and process leaders encourage accountability and get results quicker. Problem-solving leadership, training and coaching will be required for true success. Investment in time and resources is well worth the effort and cost. It will reap you rewards you can only imagine when starting out.

Process and Tools

Tools and culture go hand in hand. You need both. So jumping right in and just focusing on implementing some key Lean Sigma tools might not be the most appropriate or effective way of unleashing the power of Lean on your organisation. Getting the support and infrastructure in place upfront, planning for success, resources, etc. will save you lots of time, money and headaches down the line when it comes to actually doing the work and making the improvements.

Putting Lean Sigma ideas into action takes time, discipline and planning.

Change

"It is not necessary to change. Survival is not mandatory."

- W Edward Deming

Planning for success in any Lean Sigma deployment is essential. Having metrics to measure is vital. Infrastructure and support put in place and everyone prepared, trained in what the Lean Sigma paradigm is, what tools to use and how to use the tools properly have to be considered as well as part of your overall plan of action.

Making it the way you do business

Lean Sigma is not only about projects. It is about so much more than that. It goes deeper and beyond. It is and will become the way that you do business. Everything you undertake in your business has to start with your customers in mind - who they are, what they want and how you can get it to them quickly, correctly, in working order, exactly what they asked for and to specification, on demand, at an affordable price, delivered and guaranteed. Sounds like a tall order? Well, research shows informed, empowered customers know and get what they want.

To stay in contention, let alone be profitable and thrive, you need to have your business in line with delivering to all of the above in a cost-effective, streamlined and efficient way. With a good plan of action and the right culture, you are all set to start your deployment of Lean Sigma and unleash its power and rewards on your business, profits and customers.

Now that we have determined that Lean Sigma can actually help you eliminate waste, time, effort and material; is customer oriented; has just-in-time delivery of what they want and reduces costs while improving quality, we can look at areas of the business where Lean Sigma can help you and your customers.

Areas where Lean Can help your business

Knowing where to focus your efforts within your business is important. The 80/20 rule of thumb in Lean Sigma is a handy tool to help you prioritise and focus on what needs your attention right away. Eighty percent of the problems are usually found in 20% of the process, area or dynamic, and this is always the best place to start.

- Both business and transactional processes can benefit
- Supply chain acceleration and management

- Logistics
- Design processes
- Transactional
- Other

So far, we have discovered that Lean Sigma is:

A business management philosophy and paradigm that asks for a shift in the way we think about and do business.

It clearly stems from a proud history and grounding in the quality movement (more specifically of Japanese automakers, before spreading to Europe and the West). TQM initiatives and Toyota's early Production System put quality, time and cost and waste both in the spotlight and in clearer focus.

Getting rid of the main sources of waste in business, means paying attention to things like:

- Over-production
- Wait, lead or cycle times (start-to-finish)
- Transportation
- Processing
- Inventory
- Motion
- Scrap

There are some great tools in the Lean Sigma toolkit, four of which we mentioned initially to get you off to a good start.

The logic and rationale behind the premise and argument for Lean Sigma states that by reducing the waste, you are improving quality. As production time is lowered, costs are lowered.

Kaizen – a Japanese term (constant process focus on getting better) is at the very heart of Lean Sigma.

Lean Sigma can be helpful in many processes throughout your business, including BOTH manufacturing and transactional processes. Some, any or all of the processes involved in your business can be included in your Lean Sigma deployment and initiatives.

The key Lean Sigma principles

Getting it right the first time with no defects - identifying and solving problems from the source, quickly and as they happen.

Non value-added elimination and optimising all resources at your disposal.

KAIZEN (or continuous improvement, as it is also known) means continuously raising the bar of performance and excellence in your business. This can be done through Lean Sigma focusing in on reducing costs, improving quality, increasing productivity and better information sharing, streamlined operations and great teamwork, focused, targeted process improvement.

CUSTOMER demand drives activity in a pull, not push system and inventory, wait times etc., can be effectively trimmed and cut down (even eliminated where possible).

Extending these efficiencies and efforts to your supply chain and other business partnerships in a collaborative effort, building relationships that fit, work and last.

> Lean is basically all about getting the right things to the right place, at the right time, in the right quantity while minimising waste and being flexible and open to change.

It is like having a recipe for success in the new global, fast-paced, technology-enabled and driven, highly competitive marketplace and economy. Using the Lean Sigma way and tools better enable and empower you and your business to not only succeed in this environment, but also to flourish and thrive.

Its history and future are built on the premise that wasted, time, space, energy, effort, money and poor quality all add cost and should be made visible, dealt with and eliminated. It is not about working harder, but working quicker with less effort and waste, being efficient, consistent and with the minimum amount of waste, unnecessary movement, cost and time, Lean Sigma quickly sets you up for success and business improvement. It is about more than merely focusing on manufacturing processes. There is more to the philosophy and methodology than meets the eye.

Think of innovative ways to cut costs in your business and operation without risk to quality or customers. Eliminate any unnecessary process steps, cheaper alternatives or costly extras that are not really deemed necessary. Shared utility or tools are a great way to minimise expenses, set-up and overall costs. Make the most of the resources that you do have available.

Take a closer look at the materials and processes you and your team use every day. Do a reality check. See the costs and waste, measure everything, raise awareness of what could be done differently, more effectively and more cost-effectively.

Sometimes, process steps can be eliminated or combined to get to a result quicker and use resources, time and quality better. Standardisation goes a long way to cut down on waste.

Tweaking and adjusting machines for no apparent reason other than routine and habit should be stopped.t. Reuse, reduce, recycle comes into play. More effective materials and process steps that take less time will often help your business out, too. Find out how technology, automation, outsourcing, etc. can save you and your customers some time and money.

Kai-Zen or 'change for the better' is the mantra for Lean Sigma. It is ongoing and forever.

Taking action to correct certain aspects within your business to rid it of waste, expense and to streamline processes for optimal function and ultimate success is what Lean Sigma is all about.

Learning by doing and hands-on involvement is a great by-product and enabler of these processes and initiatives. It engages and energises. It sparks interest and builds involvement and action. Make changes, review the results and adapt if necessary. Celebrating your success and looking for new opportunity summarises this ongoing cycle well.

Kaizen, CANDO and other Lean Sigma tools

"CANDO"

C — Cleanup

A — Arranging

N — Neatness

D — Discipline

O — Ongoing Improvement

Here is an easy way to remember some of the fundamental practical things you can do right away in your business, applying Lean Sigma tools:
By effectively focusing on improving the efficiency of any underlying processes and improving performance, you will reap the financial rewards.

Bringing science, intuitive and creative problem solving, analysis and scrutiny to your business processes, you increase the handle you have on the unfolding events, steps and outcome. It drives the performance excellence of your business to new heights. Combining this approach with the discipline of process management and business process improvement tools like Six Sigma increases the impact and effectiveness.

Three pillars of strength for these business approaches are:

i.   Customer focus,
ii.   Effectiveness
iii. Efficiency

Exceeding customer expectations where you can is important. What is your niche and specialty that makes you stand out from the crowd?

Again, some self-diagnostics from the Lean Sigma toolkit can help you here regarding assessing your own business and readiness:

- How can Lean Sigma help you establish, identify and communicate that competitive edge to your business employees, partners and customers?

- How successful are your products and services in securing 'clients for life' and repeat business? How strong is your brand?

- How do you currently minimise costs, cut expenses and deal with waste?

Another important concept in Lean Sigma to grasp, understand and utilise is KANBAN. Signals or visual cues are used when customers require products, parts or services. The system is reactive and takes advantage of the 'flow' concept. On-demand solutions for operations, production lines and manufacturing facilities are suggested and preferred, due to the fact that having inventory pile up costs money, time and quality, all of which are better spent elsewhere.

Yet another essential Lean Sigma tool and utility to consider is something referred to as Total Productive Maintenance. This is different from routine or occasional maintenance that has to be performed. Having no downtime and scheduled maintenance, pro-active planning for and working with it, as opposed to a more passive-responsive approach is recommended in the Lean Sigma philosophy and practical application. It is often depicted as "deterioration prevention". It is NOT fixing machinery if and when it breaks down. The approach here needs to be more pro-active than that.

Equipment must be ready at any and all times for operation. The equipment should be able to provide you with efficiency on demand while running and provide quality service and output that can be relied upon.

Overall Equipment Effectiveness (OEE) uptime and throughput are the three key metrics you can use to track how the maintenance tasks are going and what should be done next to keep them all working as effortlessly, seamlessly individually and together as possible. Mistake-proofing is important too, reducing the variability and increasing the process capability.

We have now seen numerous examples and reasoning of why Lean Sigma will be good for your business, regardless of size, developmental phase, partners, customers, size or current level of performance. These tools can help you move your business forward.

An under-]estimated factor in all Lean Sigma deployments is the under-utilised talents of our collective and collaborative potential. We often get so busy with what each of us is doing individually that we lose sight of how much more powerful we could be if we combined our efforts.

The Importance of Measurement

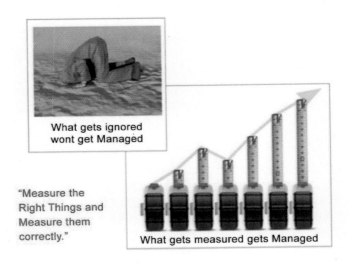

What gets ignored
wont get Managed

"Measure the
Right Things and
Measure them
correctly."

What gets measured gets Managed

At the core of Lean Sigma is:

We have to give everyone the opportunity to partake and participate, share in the experience and undertaking for maximum results.

Ask yourself how you can make the most of people's time and investment in CI or Lean Sigma practices and how it will affect/benefit your business? Your resources, employees and customers are important assets – how are you using and utilising them all in this process of becoming a more agile and cost-effective organisation/business/operation?

Always start by asking yourself the question "What can I do?" This personal hands-on approach can truly make a difference in any business.

Ways to avoid your Lean Sigma initiatives from failing or coming up short:

- Pay special attention to what the culture in your business really is. It could be totally out of alignment with the principles and fundamentals of Lean Sigma and cause stress, tension or even resistance within and throughout the organisation.

- Ask and answer yourself/your team, your business, partners and customer honestly what the existing climate is that would support (hinder/help) Lean working methods and how it will benefit stakeholders?

- Here is another useful question: Is our organisation hierarchical, rigid and autocratic and not a people-centered company?

- Learning what not to do from the mistakes and discoveries, shared learning and insights from others is critical. In LSS, there is no blame. Culture errors are opportunities to improve.

- Be aware that not everyone will necessarily share your enthusiasm for Lean Sigma. Some might have valid concerns around the implications to their current workload. Some initial resistance to any change is normal. Showing the value or the WIIFM (what is in it for me) is a very important part of the whole Lean Sigma initiative.

The TEN easy tips of how to enable Lean Sigma in your organisation

1. KEEP THE CHANNELS OF COMMUNICATION OPEN

- Talk and inform often
- Educate and empower, showcase knowledge, skill, practice and competence. Frequently invest in on-going mastery and teaching others.
- Trust, honesty and information = transparency.
- Give everyone a head start, a common language, goal and purpose.

2. GIVE OPPORTUNITY FOR EVERYONE FOR INPUT AND FEEDBACK

- Get everyone engaged, excited, hands-on, involved and aboard with your Lean Sigma initiative and plans.
- Introduce feedback and coaching, establishing communication channels.

3. CREATE AND CULTIVATE THE RIGHT WORKING CONTEXT AND ENVIRONEMENT WHERE HONESTY IS ALWAYS THE BEST POLICY

- Set communication and information sharing, learning and openness (transparency) as an organisational priority.

- Ensure that people won't feel threatened and insecure about speaking up, hiding errors for fear of embarrassment or consequences.
- Treat each other with respect and share ideas and issues openly, always keeping in mind the overall benefit (or detriment) for all if closer attention is paid to certain issues or challenges at hand.

4. TAKE NOTICE, REWARD, ENCOURAGE AND CELEBRATE.

- Select examples of great achievement with Lean Sigma, samples, project studies and specifics. Share and celebrate them with everyone. Give credit and recognition to the team where it is due for accomplishments that made a difference for the company, a specific area or problem that was solved. It is highly motivational and quite an incentive for many to keep trying and do even more.

5. Implement a system and metrics and monitor process as well as progress.

- Formalised records and tracking are essential for these Lean Sigma processes and initiative to WORK and LAST. Ensure they are streamlined, purposeful and organised, and occur regularly.

6. STICK TO THE BASICS and KEEP IT SIMPLE

- This sounds easy enough, but it is so easy to get side-tracked in the intricacies of calculations, metrics and spreadsheets that we often forget the clarity that simplicity brings.
- Making things easy to follow and stick to will help that they do exactly that.

7. STAY POSITIVE AND KEEP AT IT

8. ACHIEVE and TAP INTO YOUR RESOURCES
- Always be focusing on needs, wants, desires and motivations to mobilise and sustain momentum and change.
- Make the stake and reward personal for participating and applying the principles of Lean Sigma.
- Make it the way that you do business – without compromise.
- Set the bar and standards high; keep on reaching higher.

9. DISCIPLINED PRACTICE
- Be consistent, persistent, determined, dedicated to make things work better and last. Low cost, no waste, effective and efficient.

10. A CONTINUING JOURNEY (not only a destination)
- Ongoing learning is essential and learning from your mistakes, oversights, challenges and achievements is vital.
- Always asking what we learned, what went well, what did not work and how can we make it all better next time round should be part of normal conversation and routine.

Always remember, despite what you may have heard, there is no one-size-fits-all Lean Sigma deployment that works and fits for everyone. It depends on the organisation, leadership, dynamics, etc.

Much has been written about Lean Sigma. Practical information on how to implement Lean Sigma especially in small business is hard to come by. Tapping into the expertise of those who have walked this path is a great way to discover the secrets and pitfalls, mistakes to avoid when considering Lean Sigma for your business.

Start by asking yourself what the current readiness and knowledge levels regarding Lean would be?

For some businesses, Lean Sigma comes naturally, for others, a little more effort and discipline are required to effect and impact business processes and ensuing success.

What are you currently doing to cut down on waste, scrap or unnecessary costs?

Do you think your systems and processes are working optimally?

There is always room for improvement in any business. Lean Sigma provides us with the tools, means, channels and connections to plan, execute and sustain these changes to benefit our profit and bottom line.

Always remember that…

You cannot do everything yourself. You need the combined effort, buy-in, support and infrastructure to get things done and it may take longer than expected initially or overall, but stick with it.

Lean Sigma is an on-going journey and NOT a 'quick-fix' for business woes, although some of the tools and applications can start providing you with immediate rewards and benefits that are measurably making a difference.

Dedicated time and resources, focused and targeted effort will benefit your Lean Sigma initiative tremendously. SHIFT YOUR FOCUS MORE LONG-TERM and step out of the day-to-day fire-fighting and reduced focus we so typically have in our organisations, dealing with one problem at a time, as they come up and not following an effective overall strategy.

Lean Sigma is about more than tools, counter-intuitive thinking and application to business. It is about the people involved in, touched by, working with and through these processes and outcomes, to IMPROVE and SUSTAIN your business success and growth.

"Most of the problems are seen by your frontline employees and are unknown to management. If you're not tapping their ideas, you're missing 70-80% of the potential power of your lean journey." (Alan Robinson)

Typically management are aware of less that 5% of the actual waste in a pre-Lean Sigma organisation

Someone once quipped that LEAN IS NOT ABOUT WHAT YOU SEE, BUT COMES FROM WHAT YOU THINK. The impetus and motivation start early and

they start with each of us. Engage and enable the minds and hearts of your people and mobilise your organisation, taking it to new heights of performance excellence and increasing your bottom line profit. Tap into the collective talents within your organisation; become more organic, lead by example and emphasise that this is not a programme with a start and finish. This is an initiative that will continue, grow and expand forever, from here on forward.

Things cannot and will not stay the same with Lean Sigma – that is the one guarantee.

Skill building, training, knowledge application, refinement and mastery will come over time. There will be learning curves (often steep at the beginning), leading to lasting, proven success.

In the Lean Sigma toolbox, it is NOT ABOUT how many tools or which ones you have chosen or are/will be using, but how you unleash, utilise and leverage them.

We have covered a few key tools to get you started, but there are myriad Lean Sigma tools available and it will take time to develop your competency and mastery of any, some or all of these as part of your overall strategy of getting better as a business or organisation:

Jidoka, Kaizen, Andon, Kanban, SMED, Visual Management, 5S, 5 Whys are all examples of Lean tools that you can use. It all starts with how we think about things and the shift that we have to make in our minds from conventional, traditional and current ways we are doing things to recognising what works and what does not.

Lean Sigma demands from each of us a willingness to be open-minded; to see, discover and harness the potential savings, cost and waste reduction opportunities within and across our organisation and levels, business partners and even customers to all become more successful and better at what we do, at the lowest possible cost, without sacrificing quality.

In Kanban, it is not about the visual cue or tool as much as understanding the logic and importance of upstream and downstream process, flow and the implications for operation and the customer.

Daily decision-making, problem-solving and managing will be affected and enabled by this type of thinking and very soon it will be about so much more than mere application of tools on a couple of projects. It will change the way you think about and do business moving forward.

> Lean is not merely about what you see, lean is about how you think.

A Lean Sigma toolbox overview

A quick summary is provided here of some of the basic Lean Sigma 'tools' to get you off to a good start. They are:

5S
- Sift sweep sort sanitise and sustain
- Helps organise what's needed and eliminate what's not
- Allowing the organisation to identify problems quickly

Process mapping
- Helps to understand what it is you actually do. It allows you to see quickly the NVA and VA steps in your process

FMEA
- Allows you to measure your process
- It helps to concentrate focus on the root cause and away from the noise

3 Whys
- Problem-solving by asking why the problem occurred
- Then why that cause occurred
- Repeating the process five times until you get to the main or 'root' cause of a problem

Andon
- Operator pulls a cord that triggers a horn and a light which tells the team-leader or supervisor that he or she needs help or support
- Keep production moving and catch problems early

Jidoka
- Automation or people identifying problems
- Either stopping for correction or self-correcting PRIOR to proceeding or moving on to the next step

Kaizen
- A structured on-going process
- Engage those closest to the process
- Improve both the effectiveness and the efficiency of the process
- Remove waste and add standardisation

Kanban
- A signal or card-system that a downstream (customer) process can use
- Optimised to request a specific amount of a specific part from the upstream (supply) process

SMED
- Single Minute Exchange of Die

Visual Management
- Manage every aspect of the process
- At a glance, using visual data, signals and guides

In conclusion

Coming to grips with Lean Sigma is not always an easy task, but the initiative will soon deliver rewards to your business. Fostering its growth and filtering through all levels of the organisation will pay major dividends in the long run.

> ## "No one has more trouble, than the person who claims to have no trouble."
>
> **(Having no problems is the biggest problem of all.)**
>
> ## TAIICHI OHNO

Many of our organisations are so busy getting 'work' done, dealing with problems, fires and urgencies, meeting goals and objectives, and initiating business strategies that they do not take or have the time to even consider 'looking' for waste.

Lean Sigma leads us to pause to consider how Lean Sigma principles, rules, tools and thinking can help us with eliminating waste. Getting to root causes makes problem-solving easier and more permanent. This process is ongoing and will reveal things about your business you did not even consider. You might be surprised by what you find, unearth and reveal when using Lean Sigma thinking and tools.

Looking at processes to see how to best eliminate the different forms of MUDA or waste requires new, counter-intuitive thinking at times, a true non-traditionalist point of view.

Here is another key to really understanding the power and potential of Lean Sigma for business, regardless of their size, industry, challenges and the like:

> The ability to recognise and understand the systems that create results is not a natural ability.

We do not automatically have process focus, it is a learned skill. We have to discover, hone, harness, develop and refine it as we go through the Lean Sigma process.

See your value through the eyes and requirements of your customers and take a long hard look at what and how you are doing things to get your customers what they need and want. Look for opportunities to improve and cut down on cost, waste and expenses.

Remember – keep it simple:

> Everything that does not add value = waste

About the author Robert Potter

Robert Potter is the Managing Director at RP Consulting, a wholly owned Irish company that works to improve company profitability and customer value through implementation of operational excellence. RP Consulting specialises in executing Lean Six Sigma process and in Change Management where needed.

As a master black belt in Lean Six Sigma, Potter is also a lecturer, teacher and mentor throughout the UK and Ireland.

All RP Consulting staff are hands-on Lean consultants who have held senior roles in some of the world's most renowned companies. Their combined knowledge of Lean systems and improvement techniques has been gained through their application in all types of businesses in many market sectors from finance to manufacturing in both Ireland and throughout the world.

RP Consulting provides practical assistance to managers grappling with today's operational dilemmas through their ability to rapidly understand the current situation and then develop the appropriate approach. We actively encourage, work with and support our Client's staff to understand the situation and then to develop and implement their own solutions. In this way they can experience first-hand the immediate benefits of our just do it now approach and as a consequence we believe that their achievements will be sustained.

The time that is required for each project obviously varies dependent upon the specific organisation and its current situation, however on average our projects last 100 days and have resulted in excellent savings for our customers.

We would welcome the opportunity to earn your trust and deliver you the best service in the industry.

You can contact Robert Potter by emailing:
Robert@rpconsulting.ie

The RP Consulting Website:
http://www.rpconsulting.ie

LinkedIn Profile: http://ie.linkedin.com/in/potterrobert

Printed in Great Britain
by Amazon

23776449R00037